For My Boys

Andrea Vasser White

ROYSTON
Publishing

BK Royston Publishing
P. O. Box 4321
Jeffersonville, IN 47131
502-802-5385
http://www.bkroystonpublishing.com
bkroystonpublishing@gmail.com

© Copyright –2021

All Rights Reserved. No part of this book may be reproduced, stored in a retrieval system, or transmitted by any means without the written permission of the author.

Cover Design: Elite Book Covers
Cover Photo: Andrea Vasser White

ISBN-13: 978-1-955063-52-4

King James Version Scriptural Text – Public Domain
New International Version (NIV) - Holy Bible, New International Version®, NIV® Copyright ©1973, 1978, 1984, 2011 by Biblica, Inc.® Used by permission. All rights reserved worldwide.

Printed in the United States of America

Dedication

I dedicate this book to all those who struggle or has a loved one who struggles with a Mental Health Condition.

Just know that "You are not Alone" and there is hope.

To All those who think differently of an individual because of the color of their skin or the mental ability that doesn't measure up to your standards, then maybe your standards should change.

A Good Man

To The Father of my Boy's.

You will always be in our Hearts.

Acknowledgements

Thank you God for being a keeper. When the world said no, You said yes!

I thank my Mother Marian L. Vasser, for being by my side through everything and never giving up on me.

I thank my Boys Breyon, Steven and Devon for making me the proudest Mom on this side of Heaven

I thank my siblings Karen, Marian R, Jewel and William Vasser for letting God use you with the talents He Blessed you with

Special Thanks To:

Abi Douglas Therapist

Aiyesha Stiles APRN

Claude Drouet, LCSW Therapist

Dr F. Bruce Williams Pastor

Demetrius Stroud

Julia Royston Publishing
bkroystonreplies@gmail.com

Love you

Andrea Vasser-White

Table of Contents

Dedication	iii
Acknowledgements	v
Introduction	ix
My Life	1
2020 — What a year.	25
The Journal of My Boys	29
The Unforeseen Pandemic 2020	61

Introduction

I started writing this book for my Boy's. To give them a perspective of being a good law abiding citizen in this world that will judge them by the color of their skin. Then our lives were turned upside down like so many others by COVID, police brutality, and Mental Health Issues.
But God!

My Life

There's not much I can remember about my childhood; however, I will tell you what I can remember. I was born April 2, 1967, in Detroit, Michigan, to parents Marian (Mother) Vasser and Joe (Daddy) Vasser. I've been told, obviously because I was too young to remember, that when I was two, my parents divorced. My mother then moved back to Louisville, Kentucky, in Bible terms "from whence she came," and started a new life. Now I'm going to "fast forward" to what I can remember. OMG (and for the Baby-Boomers, that's "Oh My God!") I needed my behind beaten before I started walking. And that's an understatement! My God isn't in the mistake-making business, but if there's a chance that He made one very little, teeny, meeny, small, beany chance that He did, that would be me. But to God Be the Glory: it isn't happening. Growing up I wasn't the best child. My mother truly had her hands full. William Jewel Griffith, my granddaddy, is the only father figure I had. Boy, I'm telling you, he was the ONLY person I was scared of. So needless to say if he was around I was a perfect angel. Now, I don't remember the next set of Cookie's kids.

"Cookie" is my mother's nickname. That Karen and Marian duo came from nowhere. I promise it's one of those miraculous things that God does with making babies appearing without a man around. I don't ever recall seeing my mother with a man. Fast forward, for no reason at all, to when they we're around middle-school age. I hated their guts. I did some mean terrible things to them just because they took my spotlight. Then on top of everything, the one and only time in my entire life my daddy (whom I call Joe) bought me Christmas gifts, those two decided to catch our house on fire — and guess where the only damage was done? Just guess. Yes, you said it not me. All my Christmas gifts from Joe. Do you know the saying, "Everything happens for a reason"? Let's just say that was the beginning of my ungracious, selfish, self-centered, no clue, uneducated person that I became. Now KayKay (Karen) and Dee (Marian) may beg to differ. I'm sure they had many memories of the devil in the red dress, better than my memories. Whelp, next memory of my childhood was when I was about five, me and my cousin Tia, were over my Grandmother's house on 32nd and Virginia. My maternal grandmother and grandfather were at this time divorced. But he was out providing for his family, including Granny. Yes, the man provided for his so-called future and his past. This was so amazing to me because I had never seen a man be a provider to so many. He had his own drywall company, so he was all over Louisville doing his thing. Then he made sure each and every household close to him was taken care of. He did all home repairs including yard work, for our home, his home, my grandmother's home, and only God knows who else. So one day Tia and I were outside playing on Granny's front porch. (I would give anything to let my cousin/sister tell these stories for me, because she was my childhood ride or die.) We were one year apart in age, and we did everything together. I can't recall why, but my granny went and made ceily mad, and off I go. Let's recap: I was five, and my granny made me mad. In fact, she made me so mad, I ran away for the first time in my life. Let me tell you, at 52 years, I'm still running. Now let me back up for a minute and explain something to my sons.

Breyon, Devon, Steven, this is why I tried to knock your head off every time I saw you headed for the wrong path. I took my five-year-old self down the stairs and on to the sidewalk, as I proceeded to get to stepping. Now my grandmother said to Tia, "Let her go on. Shit, I have other things to worry about." Where was I going at five? Hell, I don't know. As you know, I was only a child. I didn't know how to come up with logical, adult decisions. All I remember was going up the stairs of my uncle's house about three miles down the road. For a five-year-old, it seemed like 130 miles. I called out my name while knocking at the door. Then I heard what sounded like a ferocious dog but was a small dog, start to bark. I ran quickly down those steps that I had so carefully climbed with my five-year-old self. Well, that plan didn't go so well, so now what??? Once again folks, I don't know — I'm only five. The next thing I remember was Mama getting home from work and looking up as she proceeded to go up the steps. Who did she see? OK, I don't want to talk about that anymore. I want to whoop my own behind right this minute, but I can't: I'm 52, and life has really caught up to me. Man, it takes my Tia Lee Buddy to tell those stories. She had to move away to Baltimore, Maryland, because my aunt met a man from there, so they got married and moved.

The next time I remember is when I was nine. I got mad at my mother for whatever reason and ran again. Although my dad was not in the picture at all, I somehow learned at a very early age that I could play my mother and dad against each other. So at nine, I decided that I was going to live with my dad in Detroit. I can't make this up; I had a cousin, during this time, that was an airline stewardess. I asked her if she could get me an airline ticket to Detroit, and she did. I'm so sorry Lord, but WTF!!!!! I mean to the 10th power! I went to Detroit, my dad's family got me enrolled into the school system, and things went really fast. I never really saw my dad when I moved to Detroit. I was either with my paternal grandmother Rosie, or her daughter, my aunt, most of the time. Well, Joe Vasser came home with a little boy one day that was my age. I asked every adult around, who is this boy? Joe took me, my cousins, and this mysterious boy to the zoo. The next thing I remember, I was back in Louisville, Kentucky, living with my mother again. I'm not sure at what point I found out "that boy" was my brother. He was exactly one month older than I was, and all this time I thought I was Joe's only child. Once again, my spotlight was taken away. I never saw my brother again, and I didn't talk to Joe till years later after I was married and had kids. Now let's pause, because that was a lot, and not even the whole story. As a parent, I'm embarrassed about my behavior as a child. And because my behavior went unpunished, I can tell you I'm still running. I run when relationships don't go the way I want them to. I run when things don't go right at work. I basically run away from anything and everything that doesn't go my way, and I don't look back. Although I'm not proud of this, I have to be transparent in order to show my boys why I'm so hard on them. You see, after my divorce, I somehow became the bad parent and my ex-husband was the fun and good parent. I had to be hard on them because I wanted them to be successful in life and not turn out like me. Now that I was a single mother, I had to work several jobs in order to provide for us.

This took a toll on me, and because of this I probably wasn't the best mom. I was so over-protective of them and I barely let them out of my sight. For this reason, my house became the hangout house. I didn't mind all their friends hanging out at my house because I for sure didn't allow them to go over to other people's houses that I didn't know. Now at some point, I noticed one particular friend rarely left our home. I didn't ask any questions; however, I did find it strange that his parents allowed him to stay at someone's house that they had never seen or talked to. I remember one day we were at the bowling alley having a family day and Steven was on his phone and was upset. As I got closer to him I could hear his father yelling at him. He was yelling so loudly I could hear him over all the bowling noise. I took the phone from him and asked what was going on. His father said he just didn't want Steven to wear out his welcome. I told him my home was Steven's home and It was not necessary for him to talk to Steven that way.

Steven was a good kid and didn't deserve that sort of treatment. From that point on, Steven was unofficially my adopted son. He stayed with us from that point on.

Now back to my life before children and marriage.

As time went on, I went to Detroit to see Joe, as much as I could. I had a family now, and it sucked the life out of me. You hear people say all the time, "when I love, I love hard." Well, that was definitely me. I loved my whole family, including KayKay and Dee (I'm rolling on the floor right now), my mother, my only brother I grew up with, and my baby sister, the one and only Jewel. My mother's last two children were my world. I loved them all so much, I took them everywhere with me. By this time I thought I was over having to have the spotlight as my goal in life, but not so much. I went away to college, which is a whole book within itself, and I discovered that my childhood demons were still there. I went away to college as an out-of-state student at Indiana University in Bloomington, Indiana. I didn't know anyone there, so I took that opportunity to rebuild my life and try to find out what my purpose was. But somehow for the first time in life I felt like I didn't fit in, and it actually bothered me. Nothing before then bothered me. So my answer for this feeling I had led me going around campus like the Tasmanian devil. I cursed everyone out for no reason at all. At the time, what I was totally unaware of, was that there was a tiny little secret about that country girl, which is what they called me because of my country accent when I talked. One of my fellow schoolmates worked as an intern at the campus clinic, and he had access to my medical file. Right before I went away to college, I went to see all of my doctors in Louisville: dentist, family doctor, and gynecologist. This was one of the reasons for my strong belief that everything happens for a reason. I got a call from the doctor informing me that I had an STD. Now with just weeks away before I go to college, I had to get this massive series of antibiotics to get cleared up. Now fortunately for me, I knew exactly where I got it from. I was only seeing one person at that time; he was the love of my life. He was my best friend and my soul mate. The one man that I actually thought I was going to marry.

When I confronted him about it, that's when he dropped the bomb on me. His response was, you couldn't have possibly gotten it from me because my other girl…. Wait, what???? Excuse me, your other girl!!! Yes, not only did he have another girl, but she was pregnant. Well, let's say that didn't end well. However, I know what you are thinking. Well, if not him, then who? I'm not sure when exactly this happened, because for a long time, which seemed like forever, I blocked it out (dissociative amnesia), but I was raped by a guy in the neighborhood. Back in the day, I was known as a tomboy. I could relate to boys more than girls. It was nothing sexual, well, not for me anyway. I just had fun with boys without all the drama girls caused. So because of this, I told myself the rape was my fault. 'What did you expect, hanging with boys I told myself?' The rape was the end of my hanging with boys. In fact, I actually hated boys. My senior year, my first — I guess you can call him — boyfriend, broke up with me. This is when I met Pookie, the man I was supposed to marry. So not only did my first boyfriend break up with me, but the guy I met at a party who I fell hard in love with, told me he had a girlfriend and a baby on the way. So to hell with all that, I went to my prom with my cousin, who happens to be a female, and we had a ball. Well, the rumors started! I told you Andrea Vasser was gay. Well, fast forward, I go to college leaving that mess of a life behind. After a few months at college, I find out that the series of meds to clear up my STD had failed. The doctors assured me that I had to have gotten it from having sex again with an infected man. Well, the problem is, I had not been with another man, so the logistics is the first one never cleared up. Now at that point, I really didn't want to be in another relationship. I was done with that. Well, I had made it through the first year in college not dating anyone. It makes sense now that nobody ever tried to get with me because of the classmate that let only God knows how many people know that I had an STD. Hell, I just thought nobody wanted me because I walked around campus cursing everybody out. I was mad as hell at the world. Right before school was to let out for the summer, a football player who lived in my dorm started talking to me and I enjoyed his company. We started dating till I found out he had sex with our star quarterback's girlfriend. Really dude, I should have stayed single. I stayed at school for the summer and took a class. There was nothing back at home for me to go to, so I stayed in Bloomington. In the middle of the summer, a friend of mine introduced me to a new incoming student who transferred from a junior college. We had a blind date at a party, then one thing led to another. We had some good times. If we were not together, we were talking on the phone till one of us fell asleep, and that was usually me. We dated, and I can't remember exactly when, but I couldn't deal with the groupies. He was on our basketball team and became famous fast. We broke things off, but really it was me running again. I really missed him because we were truly friends before we became lovers. Right before he was leaving off for the pros, he came to my apartment to visit. He wanted to know what went wrong so that he didn't make the same mistake again. I remember asking him was I still the only Black girl he had dated. He replied, "Yes, and you will definitely be the last." I tried to be hard and act like I really didn't care that he had moved on. I pulled out a magazine and told him to buy me, I believe it was, a mink coat. WHY? I didn't even wear coats!!! He left shortly after that, and I never saw him again.

Let's fast forward to my after-college life. I got married at 24 in 1991. I had my first son, December 1991, and my second son, February 1994. Things got a little complicated in my marriage, which led to a divorce in 2001. Let's pause here for a bit. Yes, it was me running once again, but, oh, how I wished someone would have sat me down and told me everything would not be peaches and cream. I was in no way prepared for marriage in any shape, form, or fashion. And it didn't help that I really had no marriages in my family as a role model. Then there's parenting, which was the hardest responsibility EVER. I couldn't juggle the two.

After the boys were grown and gone, I realized I spent the whole time raising them to understand the things they could *not* do as young Black men in America, but I never taught them what they *could* do. I taught them about white privilege because I had to let them know that there were things that they couldn't do, but Steven could because he was white. The men they have become is only by the grace of God. I'm so proud of them. They took all the good, the bad, the happy and sad, then made the best of it all. As a female, I had no idea what to teach boys. You would think all that time I spent playing with boys growing up, I would have learned a thing or two. My idea of raising good boys and keeping them out of trouble was to keep them busy at all times. No time for foolishness. I kept them in sports, and as soon as one ended, I put them in another one. Between sports, school, and church, they didn't really have time for anything else. As I look back, I see how far God has brought me — not only me, but my family as a whole. My mother raised five kids on her own and worked so many jobs to provide for us. She made it seem like raising us was so easy. I never knew an inkling of what she went through to raise us. After having kids of my own, it gave me a new lease on how I admire the best mother as far as the eye can see. I thank God for all He's brought me through. This doesn't even scratch the surface of the life of Andrea Vasser-White. But you get the idea, right?

2020 — What a Year.

Let's recap: January was a rough start, just from trying to pick up the pieces from where I left off in 2019. My sister-in-law once made the comment to me, "ReeRee, you always going through something." Those words have haunted me. I'm now 53 years old, and I still can't get this thing called life make sense. I've worked so hard for so long that I never slowed down enough to nourish myself in the Lord. Wait, is this the first time I've mentioned my life with the Lord???? What's wrong with that situation? And the funny thing is, I don't remember a time in my life being without the Lord. At an early age, I had to be responsible. By my mother working so much, I had to help with caring for my siblings. Even so, I still had no idea how hard it was to be a parent. There is no manual on parenting, marriage, or life in general. I had to learn the hard way, and I question whether I really learned at all. I feel like such a failure in every way possible. If only someone had given me just a little advice, maybe just maybe things would not have been so bad. I thought I had it all together after all; I did help raise my siblings. I made sure we were at church any time the doors were open. I was doing what I thought was right for everyone I loved. But how can I teach when I've never been taught? We have the "talk" with our children about what we think is important in life. However, do we really talk about what's important or what we think is important? Do we let our children know that nothing good comes easy? If we would take the time to let our children know the good and bad, happy and sad, ups and downs in life, maybe friendships would last, marriages wouldn't fail, and families wouldn't be turned upside down. We try to protect our kids from the ugly and bad things in this world, but if the whole truth is not told, how is one to know? My siblings all turned out fine and have made me very proud to be their "big Sissy." So in my mind, I didn't do such a bad job helping my mother raise them.

    Well, my dear sons, I will do my best to give you the necessary tools for this thing called life. While you were growing up, I wrote letters to you in case I was not around to teach you.

The letters are as follows:

To My Boys.

The Journal of My Boys

1/2/1996

You have to know that I love you more than words could ever say. You may be wondering why I'm writing this letter. Well, I don't know what the Lord has in store for me for the years to come. If it's God's will, I may be reading this letter to you when you get older. But if the Lord decides to take me on home before you are old enough to understand things, I want you to know a few things.

First of all, I want you to always treat others with the utmost respect. Matthew 7:12, Do unto others as you would have them do unto you. No matter what the situation may be, always put yourself in the other person's shoes and think how you would want to be treated if that were you. Also use this rule when you all start to date girls. Always treat a woman with your utmost respect. Women are very special; this is why God choose a woman to bear children. Treat a woman as you would have a man treat your daughter or mother. This is the most important rule of all. If you get nothing else from this letter, please always remember the Golden Rule (Matthew 7:12). You will experience a lot of negativities, unfortunately, but take all the bad that comes your way and turn it into something positive. You will have to learn to turn your head to a lot of things. The enemy will throw everything he has at you to take you *off* your game. He uses other people to do his dirty work; so see negativity for what it really is, turn to God, ask for guidance and go for a walk or do something to clear your mind. Never act *off* of emotions; nine times out of ten you will regret it later. This goes along with the scripture that says do not go to bed angry (Ephesians 4:26). So with all the issues, heartaches, and disappointments, look to God and do what's right.

The second point I want to bring to your attention is to never forget where you came from. You are from a Black race, and there are certain things about your race that you will not learn about in this country. What I mean is other people will not teach you what they don't want you to know. There are some things you have to learn on your own, and your Black heritage is one of those things. I want you to know all the good and positive things about your African heritage and not just the negative things this society wants you to believe. No matter what, always be proud of your race and who you are. The Bible tells us in Psalms 139 that people were fearfully and wonderfully made. So go with God! To help you better understand who you are and why you do the things you do, read the book *Post Traumatic Slave Syndrome* by Dr. Joy DeGruy. This will give you knowledge and help you understand racism in a different way.

Always do your best; never settle for less. Whether it be at school, work, or anything else for that matter. Being an African American Male, things definitely won't come easily for you. African Americans are considered minorities and others will try their hardest to make you inferior to them, when in reality they feel threatened by you. What I mean by this is that they make things twice as hard for you to succeed in life because they know what we are capable of, although they try to make you think differently, and they are afraid of us being more successful than they are. Just look at the news, for example. The reporters love to report all the negative things that go on in the Black community. They love to plaster the worst and paint the worst picture all over TV. And if you think about it, the more you see, the more likely it will happen because it makes you think this is the norm. Please believe me the same things happen in the white communities as well; however, because it's not reported as much, people think it just doesn't happen at all. God put us all on this Earth to do his will and His will only. No one race is better than the other in God's eyes. We should all be working together, not competing against one another. In spite of what others may say, we are all brothers and sisters through Christ; please remember this. I tell you that to say this: don't let it get the best of you when you have to work harder at something than the next person. Just give it the best you have and never give up. It is far easier to fail and give up on something than it is to achieve and succeed. Please don't ever be a failure. If you are ever put in a situation and you just can't see any way out, remember this:

> Much Prayer = Much Power
> Little Prayer = Little Power
> No Prayer = No Power

And with the frustration that goes along with working harder than your coworkers of another race can carry over into your home life. Try to prevent taking work problems home. This can lead to stress on your relationships and believe me, it will be enough of that for other reasons.

3/26/96

I want you to remember that I'm your mother and I'm also your friend. Don't ever be afraid to talk to me about anything. If I'm not around, go to the one person I was closest to. I don't care what it may concern. It could be something that you are afraid of, sex, problems you may be having with something; it doesn't matter, please talk to someone who cares and loves you. If I'm around, I will not judge you, I will only guide and help you. You are my children and I only want the best for you. We, along with God, can work through any problem. I would rather you come to me or someone who truly loves you than to go to someone who does not care for you as I do, who might lead you in the wrong direction. If by chance God takes me from this Earth and there's not another family member you trust, you can always lean and depend on God. Pray about the situation, and trust that God will see you through. Don't ever let a problem worry you to death, it's not worth it. Besides:

>Faith kills Worry
>Worry kills Faith

Which one would you rather have? Faith or worry? It's only natural for a human to be concerned about certain things, but you just have to trust in the Lord, believe me, He is in total control. There is nothing He can't handle. He only wants the best for us all. Studies show that only ten percent of things people worry about actually happen. The other ninety percent never even come to life. Also worry can send you down a dark road. If you let things get to you for so long, it will eventually affect your health. Bad and negative thoughts for a long period of time can lead to depression, anxiety, and other mental health illnesses. This then leads your body to produce certain neuron activities that in turn start to affect your overall health. The longer this goes on, the harder it is to recover health-wise. So despite the stigma of having a mental illness, if you find yourself in a situation that brings you down and you see no way out, please seek help as soon as possible. It's OK to go to a therapist, psychologist, psychiatrist, or any mental health professional for help. Take care of your mental health. This is so *very* important, because stress can literally kill you. Try to do what you can and let God do the rest. Matthew 6:34 says, "Therefore do not worry about tomorrow, for tomorrow will worry about itself. Each day has enough trouble of its own."

I also want you to always remember to never hold a grudge against another person. No matter what a person may do to you, you must always forgive them. You may find this to be a difficult thing to do because you will run into some pretty unthinkable conditions during the course of your life because you are living in a mean and cruel world where most of the time the people you will come in contact with are out for themselves and themselves only. But no matter what a person may do to you, you have to forgive them. To make it a little bit easier for you to understand, just think about all the sins you commit against God. He just keeps forgiving and forgiving and forgiving you, and you have to do the same. Besides if you don't forgive a person, you may take the risk of God not forgiving you — and isn't that a scary thought? Now that's not to say forget what someone does: there's a big difference. You forgive because God says so, but not forgetting allows you to learn from the situation and never let it happen again. You live and learn.

7/21/96

One day I hope to be able to take you all to Africa, "The Motherland," to be able to see firsthand where your ancestors are from. "Sankofa" is an African word from the Akan tribe in Ghana that means to reach back to look forward. Please try to learn as much as you can about your history. This is something you will have to do on your own because other people will purposely keep this from you because they know how powerful it would be if we all knew our history. We have a powerful and rich history. But on the same token, don't *ever* let someone tell you that you need to go back to Africa where you came from. Your ancestors came from Africa, not you! We were brought here against our will and forced to work for free. Our people built this country and have shed more blood in this country than any other race. Therefore, this is where you came from.

Please always take care of yourself spiritually, emotionally, and physically. 1) Spiritually — always keep a good relationship with God. Study the word (Bible), meditate, and pray on a daily basis, several times a day. 2) Emotionally — as I said before, no matter what you may be going through in life, don't let something keep you down. It's not the end of the world and I'm sure it's something someone else has gone through and is now doing just fine. Always have faith in God and He will see you through. 3) Physically — don't *ever* do anything to harm your body. Your body is a temple that God has blessed you with and He expects you to take care of it. If you harm your body, you harm everything else that I just mentioned. Peer pressure is a serious thing and you may come in contact with some peers that want to introduce you to drugs, alcohol, gangs, or violence. All of this was put into our community by the white man to destroy us. So far the white man is succeeding. I want you all to defeat this plan. Think highly of yourselves and know your worth. Be careful of the things you think about, because the word says in Proverbs 23:7 "As a man thinks within himself so is he." There's a good book that goes into more detail about this titled *Message 'n a Bottle: The 40 oz Scandal* by Alfred "Coach" Powell, please try to locate this and read it.

9/4/96

Always spend your time wisely. There are 24 hours in a day: eight hours for sleeping, seven to eight hours for school or work. This leaves you eight hours to do what? Let me suggest you take some time out for God. Two hours you should study the word and pray. God should be first and foremost in your life. If you keep God first, everything else will fall in place. If you shove God over to the side, your life will be a total mess. Now don't get me wrong, being a Christian does not mean your life will be trouble free. As a matter of fact, you may have more trouble than a non-Christian because Satan (the devil) wants you to stay as far away from God as possible. So, in order to keep you from God, he tries everything possible to make you unhappy hoping one day you will get frustrated with God and turn away from Him. If you think about it, it seems like people who don't follow God just don't have many problems at all. Well, why should they,

they are doing exactly what Satan wants them to do so he doesn't have to bother them. When it's all said and done with, the reward in following God can't be measured. God gives us eternal life which means in the end we will not have to suffer anymore. God loves you. He made you in His image. Satan is only out to destroy you. This is not your final destination. At some point we all will die. What you do on this Earth determines where you go after death. God's way (Heaven) or the enemy's way (hell).

Second, I think you should take some time out every day to read. You can read a book, the newspaper, a magazine: it doesn't matter what it is just read. Reading is important part of educating. You learn so much when you read. Knowledge is power, so give it about two hours. So now you're down to four hours to do whatever you please. Please spend your time wisely.

2/15/98

As you get older, you will start dating, and before you know it you will be married and having children of your own. Family is one of the hardest things I've had to deal with in my lifetime. Right now our pastor, Dr. Walter Malone Jr., is preaching a series on family. It's titled "All in the Family." I'm going to try and save these tapes for you to listen to. Having a family is a very serious issue. Having a Christian family is even more serious. Satan knows there is power in numbers. A strong Christian family is Satan's number one target. He has tried to divide families since the beginning of time, as he did with Adam and Eve. When you start to date, keep in mind the person you choose to spend the rest of your life with has to understand that there will be some good and bad times. If you are not careful, Satan will try to make the bad times outweigh the good times. That's why it's so important to keep God first in your life, not your spouse or kids. Also know that during the bad times it's not what you go through, it's how you choose to handle what you are going through.

God will turn every situation around for your good if you allow Him to.

10/28/99

Well, we are about to enter into a new millennium. I'm not sure what the future holds, but I pray that some of the things I've mentioned will help you in your life to come. I'm sure by the time you read this thing will be a whole lot different than the way it is now. Some of the things I've talked about will be old news and a whole list of other things will be happening in the world. Just keep your head up and rely on God for everything and all will be well, I promise. You are not living your life for other people; you are living for God and the purpose he has in store for you. Drown everything else out.

2/14/2001

A lot has happened since I last wrote to you. Life has not gone as planned. Your dad and I have divorced. We married young and really had no idea on how to balance work, marriage, parenting, and everything else that goes along with life. You both are young, 7 and 9, and I don't expect you to understand. This is hard for us all. The family that we once knew is no longer. We both love you no matter what and now you have two homes. You will be with your dad on the days I have to work, which is 12 hours three days a week, then with me the rest of the week. Your school, friends, and sports will all stay the same. As you get older, we will talk about this more in detail, because there are things you should know for the future in hopes that you don't make the same mistake when you become an adult.

10/20/2007

There's been so much going on in our lives. With all the hustle and bustle of getting you all back and forth to school, practice, games, and work, we barely get to talk as much as we use to. You may not understand it now, but please believe I'm doing the best I can for you. Working in the medical field has somewhat made me a monster of a parent. All the things that I see at work, I want to protect you from. Just the little things like bike accidents make me stir crazy. I have to admit, I was glad your bikes that your dad got you were stolen out of the yard. That's one less thing I have to worry about you getting hurt on. I realize I'm keeping you from enjoying your childhood, but what am I to do as a concerned Mom of young Black boys? I rarely let you stay at other friends' houses because of all the abuse I see at work. I don't mind friends staying with us, but my rules still apply. Do you remember when I let you go camping with the Boys' and Girls' club during the summer? I did this so that you could spend some time as a kid enjoying yourselves without your mean picture? Young Black boys need to physically see a successful Black man. To hear something is one thing, but to actually see it is another. This same cousin also feeds the homeless around the holidays; you can get involved with that. Or better yet, come up with your own idea for giving back. There is so much work to be done, but few who are willing. Volunteering and helping others are so rewarding and is a way for you to take your mind off of your own problems. When you see the need in the community, it makes your problems seem so small and insignificant. Someone is always way worse off than you.

I'm not sure if I've talked about

"You reap what you sow." In the Bible, there is a scripture that tells you that whatever seed you plant in the world is what will come back to you. Every human was created for God's glory and praise. He created us for companionship. As a parent, you only want the best for your child and you long for your child to love you back and obey you to the fullest. Well, so does God. He wants that from us and so much more. If we do the right thing and live the life God has in store for us, we are to serve God and serve others. This can all be summed up as karma. Karma is when life comes full circle. What goes around comes around.

What you put into the atmosphere

will come back to you. This goes for your actions as well as the words you speak

5/17/20

The power of words. God spoke this world into existence. Think about this. God gave us one mouth, and almost two of everything else. Why is this? Throughout the Bible it talks about things and situations that happened due to someone saying it. It's very important to be cautious about what you say. What you say goes into the atmosphere, then is eventually brought to life. The Bible also talks about what's in your heart will come out your mouth. So if you speak bad, talk negative, and bring people down, that's a reflection of your inner most being. This is why previously I talked about watching who you hang out with. What you surround yourself with enters into your heart. Be that person everyone wants to be like. Make a name for yourself and leave a legacy that will change the world. I have to stop here and let you all know how I smile and light up when I tell people about my boys. What a privilege it is to be your mother. I may not have been the best mom, but please know I did my best. When you become a husband, treat your wife like a queen. Hold on to the very things you experienced when you first started dating and continue to have date nights during your marriage. Learn to agree to disagree. You will have your own opinion about things but that doesn't make the other person's opinion wrong. There is always more than one way to come to a conclusion. If things become heated, step away and revisit the situation when emotions are not high. Live in the moment as if it may be your last time. Don't take anything for granted because nothing is promised.

When you have kids, love on them as much as you can. They grow so fast and the next thing you know they'll be grown and starting their own lives.

Raising you has been the joy of my life. I'm so blessed that you were good boys. I know y'all probably thought nothing you did pleased me because of all the fussing I did over the years, but it was all in love. A mother's love that will never end.

12/31/2020

Well, here we are, the last day of 2020. Wow — I'm just going to leave that thing there and reflect. Reflect on how good God is, was, and will be. I love you all with all my heart, and I'm so very proud of you. My work is done.

God Bless, Mom!

The Unforeseen Pandemic 2020

Mental health illness, or as I prefer to call it mental health conditions, are health conditions that are increasing at an alarming rate. It is my belief that all individuals deal with some sort of a mental battle within themselves at some point in time during the course of their lives. So at the time of that battle, what do you do? Well, that's one of the key factors as to how much that battle or condition takes on such a manifestation in our lives that it may determine in what direction your life (mind) goes. It is at this point where for so many, the battle becomes overwhelming.

Could the answer to this mental journey be within us? Could we somehow take total control of how the story ends? When we were created, we were equipped with everything needed to sustain life to the fullest of the power that was given to us in the very beginning. We were created not only to sustain human life, but also rule over the entire world. If we used 75% of our mental capacity, the sky's the limit as to what one could do. So if this is true, why are so many people struggling with some degree of a mental battle within?

Way before the COVID pandemic took this world by surprise, people were so caught up in the hustle and bustle of life that it at some point things became stressful instead of joyful. Busy instead of steady. Competitive instead of collaborative. Separating instead of inclusion. Hatred instead of love. I think you get the drift. Oh, what we could accomplish if only we could live by the most important law, Love thy neighbor as thyself, period! We are to love ourselves first and foremost. We are all created uniquely, pleasing in God's sight. Everyone's DNA is unique to that person, and that person only. Otherwise could you imagine how boring that would be to look at the same person everywhere you turn? All humans having the same DNA would limit how we see God, and to what He can really do. Now some would say science created everything, but God — Lord have Mercy — God has no limits as to what He can and will do. We are all different, and what God said was good, we somehow have told one another that a certain race is bad and another race should be the head of all. They allow your race to control this, and you all can have that, but you people are nothing, you never have been and you never will be, huh! And the kicker is, all of this was allowed. Humans allowed other humans to lead or take control over their land that they had managed all their lives. Could this be the start of such a growing pandemic? Think about it: You have a race who sees themselves above all. Well, a virus came along called COVID, and it didn't care who you were, where you lived, how much money you had, and so on and so forth. Now you have people who were already struggling with some sort of mental battle within for various different reasons. And now a pandemic takes the world by surprise and boy has that taken a toll on a "Well put together ordinary citizen" who has never dealt with a mental illness. Now we can go into various reasons why this mental warfare has occurred, but that's a whole book within itself. We will try to just focus on the fact that we are here now.

When an individual comes at a crossroad in life, it's not the decision they make that can lead to a mental battle within; it's how they go through it that can lead to conflict. People with high self-esteem usually coast through life with little or no problems at all. Those with moderate to low self-esteem can at times struggle with just the simplest things. And it's not usually just that one thing. Some people let small things build up inside till one day they just explode. This explosion is the start of what we call a mental breakdown. I can only speak for myself, and I'm not by any means a professional degree-wise, just by life experiences. Most doctors will say that most mental illness diagnoses are due to some sort of trauma one has experienced. Well, for me, I can truly say I'm not aware of a specific incident that took me down that dark road. I've never been diagnosed with a specific mental condition other than depression and anxiety. I never really looked at depression as a mental illness. However my body told me differently. Depression alone can literally kill you. My health went downhill fast when my depression was at its worst. Now mind you, although I've pretty much been depressed my entire life, I didn't realize it till my son developed a mental condition. It was during this time when I was seeking help for him, that someone asked me if I was doing the same for myself. Boy, if looks could kill — because in my mind that was an insult. You see, as an African American, most of us were taught "suck it up buttercup," and keep on keeping on. Nothing is wrong with you; you haven't been through anything the next person hasn't gone through. This is part of the reason so many African Americans get caught up in the vicious cycle of being institutionalized, incarcerated, homeless, then the cycle starts all over again. Now don't get me wrong; this goes for all races just not to the extent and expense of African Americans. And it's very sad that this country would rather spend billions of dollars on keeping this cycle going, rather than getting ahead of it all by educating people of these conditions, and funding different organizations that offer treatment, counseling, and various other services to meet the needs of people who are suffering.

I'm going to tell you a little bit about how my journey began. All of my life, I've felt something was wrong. But because of the stigma and lack of support, I hid my feelings and kept on moving on. I can remember several times during my life that I cried out for help, but didn't get it. At a very early age I ran away from home and as my mother would say "walk don't run," lol. I mean when I tell you I ran away I am talking from Louisville, Kentucky, to Detroit, Michigan. I did this several times. Then there was a time I attempted suicide. Now fast forward to my adult life. After I graduated from college, I got married and had two sons, and life was good, right? Not at all! I still struggled inside, but because if I said anything I would be labeled crazy, I just said nothing at all. Every now and then I would go see a psychiatrist and go to counseling but none of that ever seemed to fix me. I felt like I was all alone in this battle and nobody could possibly understand what I was going through, because let the truth be told I didn't understand, nor did I know why.

Because of me being so unhappy within, my marriage fell apart, my poor boy's had to deal with all my highs and lows sometimes within the same hour. With nobody to turn to, my life was just a total mess. I'm not even sure how, but somehow we (my boys and I) made it, Well, so we thought. When my older son went away to college, that's when our lives changed drastically. His sophomore year he started acting out of character. He started calling home a lot accusing me of doing weird things, and not just me, pretty much any person he came in contact with. Well, at first I'm thinking, "they are really messing with my son's head in Lexington." I'm wondering why they would do this to him. He is the sweetest person ever, never had a bad bone in his body. You see, he was so very intelligent and was at school on a full academic ride going into pharmacy. He was on the dean's list and doing well. But when his accusations toward me plotting against him started increasing, that's when I knew something was wrong. He was so bad off that he dropped out of school without anyone knowing it. He came back home and was living in his car because he was too ashamed to tell anyone he was no longer in school. I didn't find this out till later that during the time he was staying in his car, he was asleep in a park not too far from our house. A policeman banged on his window and startled him. Now can you imagine going through a mental breakdown not knowing what exactly is going on, then here comes a policeman that your mom has warned you about your entire life on how they treat Black people, and it happened. He was made to get out of his car, then harassed, thrown to the grown aggressively, and arrested. Well, at the time I didn't know all this but I knew something was wrong and I couldn't figure it out because I absolutely didn't know a single thing about mental health conditions. Remember I hadn't even dealt with my own at this point. Well, it took a really bad situation to occur that landed me in an institution. When my brother found out where I was, he immediately went to my son and told him now, it's your turn to get help. My immediate family were the only ones who knew a little about what my son and I were going through. But at the same time, what were any of them to do when we've all been taught to move on, this too shall pass. I wasn't sure how things would be once I got out, but my main focus was on my son's wellbeing and I knew with the state I was in, I couldn't be there for him, so I had to find someone who could be. Things got really bad before they got better. I'm telling you this journey was so exhausting that I totally don't even remember the first year or two of seeking help. When my son and I finally got diagnosed, finding the proper treatment was like trying to find a needle in a haystack. There was a waiting list to see any psychiatrist, then finding a good therapist was not an easy task. Now mind you, I'm trying to find help for the both of us. You see, not only are there very limited resources for treating mental illness, there's a huge gap between treatments in a facility, and continuing treatment once you get discharged. Well, needless to say, when I was discharged my entire being was devoted toward my son's treatment and his treatment only. This was no easy road. Not sure how, as I said before, the first two years were a big blur. Each facility would pretty much only hold you three to four days for treatment, then you were discharged to continue treatment on your own. Not only are you on your own, but you are left to find treatment in a big town with few options. For a person who is mentally unstable, this can be a bit much which leads most to just turn around and end up right where they started. So for my son, I tried to do as much for him as I possibly could. I eventually obtained POA (power of attorney) for him because he was of age during this difficult time.

    Nobody wants to talk to you when the person who needs help is of age. Frankly, I think they use this as an excuse just to be able to turn you away due to lack of personnel in that line of work. It doesn't take a rocket scientist to figure out that anyone grappling with a mental condition is not mentally in the best condition to make a mentally sane decision in most cases. If you know anyone dealing with a mental condition please know they need an advocate. I can't imagine where my son would be right now had I not fought for him. When my son was admitted to the third facility, I demanded they keep him till I found a location for him to go to where he would be able to continue to take his meds. The problem in his case was he would take meds at first after discharge, then somewhere along the line he would decide he didn't need them anymore, then we would eventually end up right back at square one. Don't ask me how, but an opening at a local halfway house became available right when my son was due to be discharged. Now I'm going to pause for a bit to explain something to you. I'm not going to push my beliefs on you, but going through something like this, you need something to hold onto to give you the strength to fight this fight trust me. For me, my strength came from God. And let me tell you, nothing but my God made things line up for me and my son during this very difficult time. Now the house my son was discharged to was the only one in our city of its kind. In this home they taught you how to become independent and responsible with your care and wellbeing. You were given your meds by a medically trained person and you had to abide by all house rules in order to stay there. This home is something that is so desperately needed in every city, and multiple ones in each city for that matter. I don't have all the answers; however, I know there need to be more help and resources for mental health treatment.

Let's think about this. If so many people really are dealing with a mental condition, why don't we hear more or know more about this? For one, you may not even see that your mental health is spiraling downhill. This was my problem for the majority of my life. It wasn't till my oldest son <u>started</u> having problems mentally that I realized I was having problems as well. As a matter of fact, during the time I was trying to get him help, several different people asked me if I was getting help. Now at first I took offense to that question being asked, but after the third, fourth, fifth, heck I can't remember which time, but after I heard that question one too many times I had to take a look at myself and my actions. I often think my untreated condition may have been a factor for what my son is going through. If only I knew what I was feeling growing up wasn't normal, and had I gotten treatment earlier in my life, maybe just maybe my son could have been spared. For two, the stigma that one carries after being diagnosed, is not such a pleasant feeling. Not only does society frown on it, at times it can be a family member or a close friend that can be your hardest letdown. You just have to go through it or see a close loved one go through it to understand. This is a forever life-changing event. This is something that, even if its treatment is successful, will be with you forever. You have to be very aware of your triggers. Take good care of yourself, because physical health plays a great deal in how your body reacts to stress or should I say, when your life doesn't go as planned. Rest is so important for brain health. If your brain doesn't naturally have some downtime, the cells in your brain go through unmanageable electrical malfunctions that if left untreated can lead to serious life threatening problems. Now I have to remind you once again, I'm not medically trained in this particular mental <u>health conversation</u>. I'm speaking from true life experiences. My only goal here is to help as many people as I can through this difficult time in the history of this country when you may feel all alone. You are not alone. It's just LIFE has taken on a new normal whether <u>you are ready</u> for it or not. And we all know change isn't easy for nobody, not this fast and this quick.

Now back to mental health. Food and nutrition are so very important. Our bodies become what we eat. Now I know a lot of you would beg to differ. I know a lot of health-conscious people who have mental health conditions. But for some, it's a combination of different things that we will later discuss, that may contribute to an illness. For others, it can be as simple as one solution. But my main focus is to help all understand that you are not alone. I'm a true believer that God puts certain people in your life for a reason, and it's *always* at the right time. I thank God for bringing Melissa Bernstein in my life when He did. She never, not one time, made me feel like I was crazy, mentally unstable, weird, or a failure. I can say whatever is on my mind around her, and never not once feel judged. She is so humble and uses her pain to help others. You can be a part of her community by going to https://www.lifelines.com/events/welcome-session.

Lifelines is exactly what it says. You have to discover what in your life brings you Joy. For Melissa, her Lifeline community goes into detail on how to discover your lifeline. For me, I have several lifelines. I'll start with nature. Being in nature, around all God's creation, is so serene for me. Just being with God alone is my lifeline. He alone makes everything all right. But being in nature reminds me of how magnificent my God is and there's nothing He can't do. For you, you just have to reach deep within and find what brings you Joy. Trust me I know when it seems so dark, you may not be able to remember a happy time in your life. But the truth is, you're still here. There is something that has <u>kept you</u> going, and obviously your time is not up yet. There's something you have to do, to help others as well as yourself.

Your mission is not complete until God says it is, so you might as well figure out your passion, go for it and enjoy the ride. Life is not meant for you to be down and out. Although those down and out days make you stronger as long as you don't waddle in it for <u>too long</u>. Your down or not-so-good days could be the very experience you can share to help someone else. Oh the joy in helping others.

Sometimes when I'm having a not-so-good day, many of those days someone I may or may not know talks to me about what they are going through. In my head I'm saying, really, do you want to hear my problems? But as I reflect back to when something like this happens, I can usually give advice from my life experience and feel the joy it brings to see a smile on someone's face at the end of the conversation.

For so long I felt all alone, and

didn't think anybody would ever understand what I was going through and why, because I didn't even know. After my divorce in 2001, things for me got worse. After lashing out several times at my coworkers, my director at work knew I was out of character and recommended I go seek counseling. What a disgrace, but I knew he was right. I tried therapy several times with several different people and things never got better for me until 2014 when my son started having mental issues. I was so devastated, and I knew in order to help him, I had to help myself. Now this is the hardest part of all. Trying to find the right fit.

Unfortunately the demand for

mental health specialists is far greater than what's available. And not all the help that's out there is there for your best interest. For me, it took about a year or two to find a psychiatrist and therapist that worked for my son and me. And what worked for him, didn't work for me, so we go to different specialists. If it's you that's looking for help, please don't give up. There is someone for everyone; you just have to find them. If you are looking for a loved one, same thing, don't give up because this definitely is not going to be easy, especially if your loved one is of age. A minor, not so much. With my son, I first had to get POA. This gives you legal rights to speak on their behalf. The most important thing I want you to take from this is that this process may not be easy, but don't give up. Keep searching till you find someone you feel comfortable with.

I can't stress enough how important it is to take time out and check on your mental health. Just like you get an annual physical health checkup, you need to get a mental health checkup. Mind and body work together. So take care of both.

Surround yourself with people who understand you and your condition. This is your safe space. Your safe space is where you can go and talk with someone you trust. Someone who knows your treatment plan and will be able to help you get back on track. For me, this is a daily routine. My day can start so good, and at some course of the day I may hear , see, do or feel something that takes me down that dark road. Ex: My son's purchased me a laptop to help me with my volunteer work services. I currently have to go to the library for various reasons. Well the library is definitely not what it used to be. I remember growing up that once you entered the library, not a word is to be said. And if by chance you really needed to say something, it was a very quiet whisper. Well not so much now. I've been to pretty much every library in Louisville and it's like being at work. Conversations are as if what you would expect in your place of business. Then there's the COVID effects of a person's mental health that is on the rise. I have been to some of the libraries in the suburbs and I'm talking people are just vary inconsiderate. One woman came in the library with her two small children. They didn't even look to be school age. When she entered the library, she was asked to wear a mask by a staff member. Let's just say, that situation got so out of hand, that I packed up and left. That totally ruined my day. I went home and cried.

I then lashed out on my boys. I told them after all I've done for them, the least they could do was get together and purchase me a laptop so that I didn't have to be subjected to what I just experienced. They did just that. I got the work. Your Best Life is to come. Don't let your circumstances determine your Destiny. That fact that you're still here means that you have work to do. My work is to bring awareness to the importance of good Mental Health. Will you join me?

www.ingramcontent.com/pod-product-compliance
Lightning Source LLC
LaVergne TN
LVHW021408080426
835508LV00020B/2494